A PRAYER GUIDE FOR CHURCH INTERCESSORS

31 Days of Prayer

by

Latasha R. Brown

*Strategic Ways to Pray and Decree to get results in your
local church to advance the Kingdom of God*

Table of Contents

A PRAYER GUIDE FOR CHURCH INTERCESSORS

31 Days of Prayer

by

Latasha R. Brown

*Strategic Ways to Pray and Decree to get results in your
local church to advance the Kingdom of God*

Table of Contents

Introduction

This book is designed to help lay servants that are new to prayer and intercession in ministry. It's the first step for those that don't know where to begin in their journey of praying for their church, community, Pastors and leaders. This book will guide you on how to pray God's Word, believing God's Word and decreeing God's Word. You will become skilled in your prayers as you use this book as a guide. We as Believers, have to understand there is life and death in the power of the tongue. However, we quickly forget or never read the rest of that scripture; a man shall eat good by the fruit of his mouth, and that God creates the fruit of the lips (Proverbs 18:21).

I remember my husband starting a new ministry in 2011 with just six people. All of us knew to pray. However, only a few of us knew the importance of prayer. We prayed daily for the church and other churches open in the name of the Lord. However, the more I prayed, I began to realize it was more needed. I noticed my prayers and some of the others praying with me, we were repeating the same things in our prayers. I desired more in prayer with the Lord but didn't know how or where to start. It wasn't until I was in meditation) with Holy Spirit that He began to speak to my heart about how I was praying.

Holy Spirit acknowledged my emotions, encouraged and spoke the Word - Jeremiah 1:12 to my heart. Holy Spirit, in His soft voice said, "You're praying from your emotions and what you think your Pastor and the church needs, but the Lord watches over His Word to perform it." Now it is nine years later, and Holy Spirit has taught me how to partner with Him and what to pray for concerning my church and for leadership.

This book is the outgrowth of many hours spent in morning prayer and meditation with God. Additionally, this book is the overflow of hosting a weekly prayer call for women for over seven years. Lastly, this book was produced after my Pastor petitioned our church to 31 days of prayer. As I embraced the assignment to pray for 31 days, I began to immediately ask Holy Spirit what we as Intercessors and the Body of Christ should pray. In this book, is the 31 topics Holy Spirit led us to pray for the church to advance His Kingdom.

Therefore, I pray you, yes you, new intercessor, lay servant, minister, deacon, armor bearer, minister in training and Believer will use this manual as a new discipline of praying effectively. Take your place confidently, as a *house of prayer*. God is waiting on you to partner with Holy Spirit to speak, believe and decree in building your local church, community, region, nation, and church leaders.

How To Use This Guide

I don't know how and when your prayer teams meet. Maybe, weekly, biweekly or monthly, however whenever they do meet there should be order and protocol. What you will find in this prayer manual are prayers written for you and your team to pray daily for your church, community and your leader's specific vision.

Once you gather as a team/ministry, begin to speak the Word of God out of your mouth so that it can get in your heart. Speaking and praying the Word brings confidence to you. You will begin to realize you are not working or praying in your strength, but the strength of Holy Spirit. This prayer guide has spiritual instructions that will help initiate, stir up, grow, and develop you as a person of prayer.

As you begin to pray the targeted prayer, you then should allow Holy Spirit to guide your prayer from there. This will help you to distinguish between your head and your heart. Again, the targeted prayers in this guide is a blueprint to help guide and propel you into true intercession. At the end of each daily prayer is a reflection page for you to share what Holy Spirit is saying to you.

Holy Spirit

I f you want to become a skilled intercessor or person of prayer, you are going to have to become one with Holy Spirit. He is the third person of the God. God is Father, Son and Holy Spirit. And all the divine traits are attributed to the Father and the Son which are equally attributed to Holy Spirit.

He is referred to as a person by scripture. According to John 14:16 *"But the Comforter, which is the Holy Spirit, whom the Father will send in my name, he shall teach you all things" KJV.* Therefore, Holy Spirit is the true teacher and guide of your prayer and prayer language. This guide is giving you a rigid prescribed formula for prayer, but it is Holy Spirit who will lead and teach you to pray for your church and leader from your heart.

Holy Spirit is also a gift according to Luke 11:11-13, "Which of you fathers, if your son asks for a fish, will give him a snake instead. Or if he asks for an egg, will give him a scorpion? If you then, though you are evil, know how to give good gifts to your children, how much more will you Father in heaven give the Holy Spirit to those who ask him" KJV. I know you may be thinking, I never thought of Holy Spirit as a gift. Well, now is the time moving forward that you do so. What normally happens when you receive a gift? Yes, we are thinking the same…happy! And we use the gift that is given to us. So, what are you waiting for?

As a born-again believer, I want to encourage you, you have the desire on the inside of you to let communication flow from your heart to God. I don't care if you just joined the intercessor team today, just accepted your call to preach the Gospel or is just a lay servant that wants more of God, Holy Spirit will guide you. Praying in the Spirit means to follow the leadership of Holy Spirit and pray as He directs you. That's why at the end of each formulated prayer, Holy Spirit should have stood up on the inside of you and directed you specifically to pray.

Getting to know Holy Spirit is like getting to know anyone else, you have to spend time with Him. Let Him guide and teach you. I urge you to take this gift, if you haven't! He is the secret to moving from praying the pages of this guide to the heart of the Father.

Prayer 101

I know you're thinking prayer is for the pastor, the ministers in training, the elders or even the 1st Lady. Please get that myth out of my mind and heart. In John 15:7, *"But if you remain in me and my words remain in you, you may ask for anything you want, and it will be granted" NLT*, this sounds like prayer to me. Therefore, if you are a believer you abide or remain in Him and He in you and whatever you ask or hope for it will be done through prayer.

When we pray, we are implementing the victory over Satan that was won at the Cross. Prayer is one of the ways we release the will of God upon the earth. That's why you, intercessors, lay servant, babe in Christ, ministers have the power to serve your local church by being used by God with the help of Holy Spirit to pray things through. That is why this guide has much of the Word in it, because you can't pray without the Word of God. Prayer and the Word must be combined.

Reading, studying and meditating on the promises of God will motivate you to pray. Praying the Word of God will expand your vocabulary and ability to pray. When you pray, you are reinforcing the fact that principalities and powers have been spoiled according to Colossians 2:15, *"In this way, he disarmed the spiritual rulers and authorities. He shamed them publicly by his victory over them on the cross" NLT.*

Prayer doesn't have to be hard, just start where you are. You know and feel Holy Spirit burdening you to pray at another level. Don't let Mother Johnson and Deacon Smith's prayers put you in fear. There is a sound from you God wants to hear. Don't compare yourself to others in the church. Pray at the capacity the Lord has given you and Holy Spirit will do the rest. Stop thinking your prayers, tongues, and anointing has to match your leader's or the top intercessors.

DAY 1
Unity in Church

Father in the name of Jesus, as your Word says in 1 John 5 this is the confidence that we (**church name**) have in you; that if we ask anything according to your will, you hear us therefore we pray for unity and harmony within (**church name**) other churches, schools, businesses, families, city and country.

Father reunite your Body of believers, for you said in your Word in Psalm 133, "It is *good* and *pleasant* for brethren to dwell together in unity." Therefore, let (**church name**) dwell in unity and love in the name of Jesus.

Father in the name of Jesus, we the members of (**church name**) commit to praying for one another and loving one another in spite of offense and misunderstanding. We bind the spirit of offense, hurt, jealously, and pettiness. I pray that we will hold each other accountable in love.

We bind as your Word says in Ephesians 4:31, "Let all bitterness, wrath, anger, outburst, and blasphemies with all malice be taken away from you in the name of Jesus."

I bind the spirit of gossip, unforgiveness, arguing, revenge, adultery, retaliation, hatred, stubbornness, rebellion, kicking against leadership and phonies in the name of Jesus within (**church name**).

Father in the name of Jesus, we pray that (**church name**) will come together concerning everything Pastor _____'s vision includes for the year _____. We pray for harmony during worship service, Bible Study, Projects, First Fruit Sunday and all outreach, services and events.

Father in the name of Jesus, we pray as members of the body of Christ, we will worship in harmony, fellowship in harmony, sing in harmony and live in harmony with the fruit of the spirit according to Galatians 5:22. I loose – love [unselfish concern for others], joy, [inner] peace, patience [not the ability to wait, but how we act while waiting], kindness, goodness, faithfulness, **23** gentleness, self-control in the name of Jesus.

Father in the name of Jesus, help us at (**church name**) and others to be like-minded and on one accord in love, joy, peace, prayer, giving, serving, and worshiping.

We decree and declare 1 Corinthians 1:10 Amp - all believers, by the name of our Lord Jesus Christ, that all of us be in full agreement in what we say, and that there be NO divisions *or* factions among us church leaders, deacons and elders but that we be perfectly united in our way of thinking and in our judgment. In Jesus name. Amen.

Prayer Reflection

Now that the Holy Spirit is stirring within you, it is your opportunity for the Holy Spirit to flow prophetically through you. Write what He is saying concerning unity in your church now.

_____

_____

_____

_____

_____

_____

_____

_____

_____

_____

_____

_____

_____

_____

_____

_____

_____

_____

_____

_____

DAY 2
Unity in Marriage

Father in the name of Jesus, we pray every husband will provide Godly leadership to their wives the way Christ does the church in the name of Jesus.

Father we pray in the name of Jesus that every marriage will walk in harmony and love through the power of the Holy Spirit according to Mark 10:9.

Father we pray in the name of Jesus that every marriage in (**church name**) will grow stronger day by day and live in integrity to one another.

We decree and declare Father God that every husband will cherish his wife and only his wife according to Ephesians 5:25.

We decree and declare every husband in (**church name**) will honor and delight in his wife as in Ephesians 5:25.

We decree and declare every husband will take responsibility for his family in the name of Jesus.

We decree and declare every husband will arise and call his wife blessed and praise her as in Proverbs 31.

We decree and declare husbands will come home to their wife faithfully every day in the name of Jesus.

We decree and declare every husband will take responsibility for his family in the name of Jesus.

We decree and declare every husband and wife will continue to become one flesh according to Matthew 19:6.

We decree and declare every wife will support her husband in ways that show support for Christ.

We decree and declare every husband will only have eyes for his wife in (church name) in the name of Jesus.

We decree and declare every wife will only have eyes for her husband in (church name) in the name of Jesus.

We decree and declare every wife will submit unto her own husband as unto the Lord according to Ephesians 5:23.

We decree and declare every wife will respond in love, gentleness and display inner beauty towards their husband in the name of Jesus.

Father in the name of Jesus, we come against divorce, separation and infidelity in marriages.

Father, we pray according to your Word in Hebrews 13:4 that all marriages in (**church name**) are kept honorable and every marriage bed kept pure in the name of Jesus.

We bind instability in marriage.

We bind a spirit of fantasy thinking in marriage.

We bind emotional and physical affairs in marriage.

We bind lustful thinking in marriage.

We bind unforgiveness in marriage.

We bind pornography in marriage.

We bind every Jezebel seducing spirit targeted towards husbands and wives.

We bind every generational curse in marriages in (**church name**).

We bind the spirit of confusion in marriage.

We loose faithfulness in marriage.

We loose stability in marriage.

We loose loyalty in marriage.

We loose true covenant in marriage.

We decree and declare every wife is pure in her marriage to her husband in the name of Jesus.

We decree and declare every husband is pure in his marriage to his wife in the name of Jesus.

We decree and declare emotional healing to every husband and every wife in **(church name)**.

We decree and declare Kingdom families and Kingdom marriages in **(church name)**.

Prayer Reflection

Now that the Holy Spirit is stirring within you, it is your opportunity for the Holy Spirit to flow prophetically through you. Write what He is saying concerning marriages in your church now.

_____

_____

_____

_____

_____

_____

_____

_____

_____

_____

_____

_____

_____

_____

_____

DAY 3
Single Men & Women

Father in the name of Jesus, we pray for every man and woman in the Body of Christ. We pray that they will care for the things of the Lord as your Word says in 1 Corinthians 7:32 on how they can please the Lord.

We pray every single man and woman in (**church name**) will abide in your Word holding fast to Pastor _____'s teachings and living in accordance with the Word.

We pray their hearts be made pure for out of an evil heart comes fornication.

We pray every single man and woman will always pray and not give up, lose heart, faint or settle for less than God's very best for his or her future/life in the name of Jesus.

We decree and declare the world's systems will have no influence on their desires or lifestyle in the name of Jesus.

We decree and declare every single man and woman will completely surrender their life to the Lord in order for God to bring their future husband and/or wife according Jeremiah 29:11 in the name of Jesus.

We decree and declare every single man and woman in (**church name**) will trust God in choosing their future mate for them according to Proverb 3:5-6

We decree and declare every single man and woman in the body of Christ has everything thing they need according to Psalm 23:1. They will not look for another woman or man to supply their needs in the name of Jesus.

We decree and declare God's goodness and mercy shall follow them during their singleness and the rest of their lives according to Psalm 23:6 in the name of Jesus.

We decree and declare every single man and woman will lay aside every weight and sin according to Hebrews 12:1 in the name of Jesus.

13

Father in the name of Jesus, we pray for emotional and psychological healing for every single man and woman in (**church name**)

We bind a painful past in the name of Jesus.

We bind the spirit of grief in the name of Jesus.

We bind the spirit of unforgiveness in the name of Jesus.

We bind blocked emotions in the name of Jesus.

We bind deep hurt in the name of Jesus.

We bind man sharing in the name of Jesus.

We bind fear of being alone in the name of Jesus.

We bind rage and anger in the name of Jesus.

We bind the spirit of torment in the name of Jesus.

We bind a spirit of envy and jealously in the name of Jesus.

We bind a spirit of masturbation in the name of Jesus.

We bind a spirit of bitterness in the name of Jesus.

We bind isolation and idleness in the name of Jesus.

We bind the spirit of rejection in the name of Jesus.

We loose love in the name of Jesus.

We loose the peace of God in the name of Jesus.

We loose self-esteem and self-confidence in the name of Jesus.

We loose the joy of the Lord in the name of Jesus.

We loose God's righteousness in the name of Jesus.

We loose holiness and purity in the name of Jesus.

We loose a sound mind in the name of Jesus.

We loose temperance and kindness in the name of Jesus.

We decree and declare every single man and woman is transformed by the renewing of their minds in Christ Jesus according to Romans 12:1. God bring their thoughts into obedience with your Word.

Prayer Reflection

Now here is your opportunity for the Holy Spirit to flow prophetically through you. Write what He is saying concerning the single men and women in your church now.

_____

_____

_____

_____

_____

_____

_____

_____

_____

_____

_____

_____

_____

_____

_____

_____

DAY 4

Father in the name of Jesus, we pray for every man **(church name)** in the name of Jesus. We pray that every man they will care for the things of the Lord as your Word says in 1 Corinthians 7:32 on how they can please the Lord.

We pray every single man in **(church name)** will abide in your Word holding fast to Pastor _____'s teachings and living in accordance with the Word.

We pray every single man will always pray and not give up, lose heart, faint or settle for less than God's very best in **(church name)** for his or her future/life in the name of Jesus.

We decree and declare the world's systems will have no influence on the men in **(church name)**, neither their desires nor lifestyle in the name of Jesus.

We decree and declare every man will completely surrender their lives in **(church name)** according to Jeremiah 29:11 in the name of Jesus.

We decree and declare every man in **(church name)** will trust God in all of their ways according to Proverb 3:5-6 in the name of Jesus.

We decree and declare every man in **(church name)** has everything thing they need according to Psalm 23:1. They will only look for to supply their needs in the name of Jesus.

We decree and declare God's goodness and mercy shall follow every man in **(church name)** and the rest of their lives according to Psalm 23:6 in the name of Jesus.

We decree and declare every single man will lay aside every weight and sin **in (church name)** according to Hebrews 12:1 in the name of Jesus.

Father in the name of Jesus, we pray for emotional and psychological healing for every man in **(church name)** in the name of Jesus

We bind a painful past in the name of Jesus.

We bind the spirit of grief in the name of Jesus.

We bind the spirit of unforgiveness in the name of Jesus.

We bind blocked emotions in the name of Jesus.

We bind deep hurt in the name of Jesus.

We bind fear of being alone in the name of Jesus.

We bind rage and anger in the name of Jesus.

We bind the spirit of torment in the name of Jesus.

We bind a spirit of envy and jealously in the name of Jesus.

We bind a spirit of masturbation in the name of Jesus.

We bind a spirit of bitterness in the name of Jesus.

We bind isolation and idleness in the name of Jesus.

We bind the spirit of rejection in the name of Jesus.

We loose love in the name of Jesus.

We loose the peace of God in the name of Jesus.

We loose self-esteem and self-confidence in the name of Jesus.

We loose the joy of the Lord in the name of Jesus.

We loose God's righteousness in the name of Jesus.

We loose holiness and purity in the name of Jesus.

We loose a sound mind in the name of Jesus.

We loose temperance and kindness in the name of Jesus.

Prayer Reflection

Now here is your opportunity for the Holy Spirit to flow prophetically through you. Write what He is saying concerning the men in your church now.

_____

_____

_____

_____

_____

_____

_____

_____

_____

_____

_____

_____

_____

_____

_____

_____

DAY 5
Children

Father in the name of Jesus, I pray and confess your Word over every child in (**church name**).

I pray every parent and grandparent will cast their cares concerning their children on you Father God, according to 1 Peter 5:7 in the name of Jesus.

I decree and declare our children of (**church name**) minds and memory are blessed and receive good grades according to Proverbs 10:7 in the name of Jesus.

I decree and declare that our children in (**church name**) obey their parents in the Lord as because it is right according to Ephesians 6:1 in the name of Jesus.

I decree and declare our children will grow strong in the Lord in the name of Jesus.

I decree and declare our children are filled with wisdom from the Lord in the name of Jesus.

I decree and declare our children of (**church name**) will follow the voice of their parents and God and a stranger's voice they will not follow according to St. John 10:5 in the name of Jesus. I pray they will flee from the enemy in Jesus' name.

I decree and declare our children of (**church name**) are taught of the Lord and shall receive much peace in their lives according to Isaiah 54:13 in the name of Jesus.

I decree and declare our children in (**church name**) love you Lord in the name of Jesus.

I decree and declare You give Your angels charge to cover our children (**say their names**) in the name of Jesus.

I bind racial profiling for all children in the name of Jesus.

I bind peer pressure against our children in (**church name**) in the name of Jesus.

I bind defeat over our children in the name of Jesus.

I bind bullying over our children in the name of Jesus.

I bind the spirit of ADD/ADHD in our children in the name of Jesus.

I bind a spirit of defiant behavior, negative hyperactivity and tantrums in the name of Jesus.

I loose fairness and justice over our children in the name of Jesus.

I loose protection in the name of Jesus.

I loose obedience in the name of Jesus.

I loose purity in the name of Jesus.

I loose wisdom in the name of Jesus.

I loose a sound mind over our children in the name of Jesus.

Latasha R. Brown

Prayer Reflection

Now that the Holy Spirit is stirring within you, it is your opportunity for the Holy Spirit to flow prophetically through you. Write what He is saying concerning the children in your church now.

_____

_____

_____

_____

_____

_____

_____

_____

_____

_____

_____

_____

_____

_____

_____

_____

_____

DAY 6
Single Mothers & Fathers

Father in the name of Jesus, I pray wisdom and direction for every single father and mother.

I decree and declare God will be a father to help single fathers and mothers raise their children according to Psalm 68:5.

I decree and declare every single father and mother will "arise, and lift up their lad, and hold him with your hand, for God will make him a great nation" according to Genesis 21:18 in the name of Jesus.

I decree and declare God will provide every need for every single father and mother to fully take care of their children according to Philippians 4:19 in the name of Jesus.

I decree and declare every single father and mother provides for their children.

I decree and declare the steps of a single father and mother are ordered by the Lord on raising their child(ren) according to Psalm 37:23 in the name of Jesus.

I decree and declare every single father and mother will carry their heavy load concerning their children and everyday struggles to the Lord in return for His rest according to Matthew 11:28 in the name of Jesus.

I bind the spirit of worry over every single father and mother in the name of Jesus.

I bind the spirit of fear of single fathers and mothers raising their children in the city of _____ from drugs, gang affiliation, sexism and racism in the name of Jesus.

I bind helplessness of every father and mother in (**church name**) as they raise their children in the name of Jesus.

I loose rest in the name of Jesus.

I loose peace in the name of Jesus.

I loose confidence in the Lord in the name of Jesus.

I loose child support in the name of Jesus.

I loose strength in the name of Jesus.

I loose patience in the name of Jesus.

Prayer Reflection

Now that the Holy Spirit is stirring within you, it is your opportunity for the Holy Spirit to flow prophetically through you. Write what He is saying concerning single mothers and fathers your church now.

_____

_____

_____

_____

_____

_____

_____

_____

_____

_____

_____

_____

_____

_____

DAY 7
Church Leadership

Father in the name of Jesus, I pray for every apostle, pastor, teacher, prophet and evangelist will humbly continue to equip and build the body of Christ according to Ephesians 4:11-12 in the name of Jesus.

Father in the name of Jesus, I pray the seven-fold anointing over all church leaders of (**church name**) according to Isaiah 11:2.

Father in the name of Jesus, I pray God's guidance and wisdom for every deacon, minister, elder and associate pastor in (**church name**) in the name of Jesus.

I decree and declare every leader of (**church name**) will pray without ceasing for our Pastor _____ in the name of Jesus.

I decree and declare all leaders are committed to the vision you have given Pastor _____ of (**church name**) in the name of Jesus.

I decree and declare all leaders of (**church name**) will never speak against Pastor _____ in the name of Jesus.

I decree and declare church leaders of (**church name**) will walk by Faith and not by sight according to 2 Corinthians 5:7 in the name of Jesus.

I decree and declare every church leader will walk after the Spirit man concerning his and her brothers and sisters in the congregation and not after the flesh because the flesh profiteth nothing according to St. John 6:63 in the name of Jesus.

I decree and declare all leaders of (**church name**) are striving to walk in holiness and blameless before the Lord according to Genesis 17:1 in the name of Jesus. They are leaders that are a part of the Abrahamic covenant in the name of Jesus!

I decree and declare every church leader will put feet to Pastor _____'s vision to advance the Kingdom of God in the name of Jesus.

I decree and declare every church leader in (**church name**) is a 100% tithes and offering payer in the name of Jesus.

I bind inconsistency in church leaders in the name of Jesus.

I bind discord and division among church leaders in the name of Jesus.

I bind a spirit of pride in church leaders in the name of Jesus.

I bind a spirit of religion in church leaders in the name of Jesus.

I bind a Jezebel spirit of manipulation and domination in church leaders in the name of Jesus.

I bind the spirit of offense in church leaders in the name of Jesus.

I bind any hidden agendas in church leaders in the name of Jesus.

I bind double-minded church leaders in the name of Jesus.

I loose the right people serving in ministry in the name of Jesus.

I loose unity among leaders in (**church name**) in the name of Jesus.

I loose a spirit of humility among every church leader in (**church name**) in the name of Jesus.

I loose flexibility in church leaders in the name of Jesus.

I loose diligence within church leaders in the name of Jesus.

I loose the blood of Jesus over their children and families in the name of Jesus.

I loose single-minded church leaders in the name of Jesus.

Prayer Reflection

Now that the Holy Spirit is stirring within you, it is your opportunity for the Holy Spirit to flow prophetically through you. Write what He is saying concerning church leadership your church now.

_____

_____

_____

_____

_____

_____

_____

_____

_____

_____

_____

_____

_____

_____

_____

_____

_____

DAY 8

Pastor's Vision for (church name)

Father in the name of Jesus, we thank you that (**church name**) is experiencing the goodness, grace and mercy from the Lord.

Father in the name of Jesus, we thank you that (**church name**) is redeemed from poverty, sickness and spiritual death according to Galatians 3:13.

Father in the name of Jesus, make your grace abound toward your people. Bless them with good and stable jobs and careers. Bless them with a willingness and ability to give their tithes and offerings with a generous and cheerful heart according to 2 Corinthians 9:6-10.

Father in the name of Jesus, let your people praise you for your goodness Lord and your wonderful works to the children of men.

I decree and declare every member of (**church name**) are living under an open heaven in the name of Jesus. Amen.

Prayer Reflection

Because this prayer is specific to each leader, below you can ask your Pastor/Bishop his or her vision and pray it through according to the Word of God.

_____

_____

_____

_____

_____

_____

_____

_____

_____

_____

_____

_____

_____

_____

_____

_____

DAY 9

Husbands

Father in the name of Jesus, give grace to every husband to honor his wife.

Father in the name of Jesus, teach each husband how to love his wife as you love your bride, the Church.

Father in the name of Jesus, strengthen each husband of (**church name**) to rule his own house well, provide godly headship and financial stability for his family.

Father in the name of Jesus, let every husband be faithful to his one wife you have given him.

Father in the name of Jesus, let every husband never grow bitter toward his wife according to Colossians 3:19.

We decree and declare every husband in (**church name**) will honor and delight in his wife as Ephesians 5:25.

We decree and declare every husband will take responsibility for his family in the name of Jesus.

We decree and declare every husband will arise and call his wife blessed and praise her as Proverbs 31.

Prayer Reflection

Now that the Holy Spirit is stirring within you, it is your opportunity for the Holy Spirit to flow prophetically through you. Write what He is saying concerning church leadership your church now.

_____

_____

_____

_____

_____

_____

_____

_____

_____

_____

_____

_____

_____

_____

_____

_____

DAY 10
Emotional Healing

Father in the name of Jesus, thank you for healing the brokenhearted in **(church name)** and binding up their wounds according to Psalm 147:3.

Father in the name of Jesus, we receive your rest for those of us that have been heavy laden with emotional stressors.

Father in the name of Jesus, thank you that you wish above all things that we at **(church name)** will prosper and be in good health even as our souls prospers.

I bind every evil spirit that has come into our lives in the name of Jesus.

I bind every spirit of hurt, rejection, shame, guilt, and offense in the name of Jesus.

I bind every spirit traumatic experience in my childhood in the name of Jesus.

I bind every negative spirit in my past in the name of Jesus.

I bind every spirit of rape and molestation in the name of Jesus.

I bind blocked emotions in the name of Jesus.

I bind deep hurt in the name of Jesus.

Prayer Reflection

Now that the Holy Spirit is stirring within you, it is your opportunity for the Holy Spirit to flow prophetically through you. Write what He is saying concerning your emotional healing now.

_____

_____

_____

_____

_____

_____

_____

_____

_____

_____

_____

_____

_____

_____

_____

_____

_____

DAY 11
City & Government Officials

Father in the name of Jesus, we pray your people, who are called by your name, will humble themselves and pray and seek your face and turn from their wick ways and then you will heal our land according to 2 Chronicles 7:14. If my people who are called by my name humble themselves, and pray and seek my face and turn from their wicked ways, then I will hear from heaven and will forgive their sin and heal their land. (Did you mean to put the actual scripture and the paraphrase here?)

Father in the name of Jesus, establish your justice and make the wrong things right in our nation, city, community and church leadership.

Father in the name of Jesus, we decree and declare that Jesus is Lord over (**name your city and state**).

Father in the name of Jesus, thank you that you have delivered us, the city of (**name your city**), and out of the enemy's hand.

Father in the name of Jesus, thank you that our alderman, mayor and city officials will role model integrity, Godly wisdom and authentic leadership to the city of (**name your city**).

I decree and declare angels be released over our city of (**name your city**).

I decree and declare an outpouring of Holy Spirit over (**name your city**) in the name of Jesus.

I bind the spirit of mental illness in the city of _____.

I bind the spirit of greed and control in the city of _____.

I bind the spirit of crime and gang violence in the city of _____.

I loose restoration in the minds in the city of (**name your city**) in the name of Jesus.

I loose love and the spirit of submission in the city of (**name your city**) in the name of Jesus.

I loose peace in the city of (name your city) in Jesus name.

Prayer Reflection

Now that the Holy Spirit is stirring within you, it is your opportunity for the Holy Spirit to flow prophetically through you. Write what He is saying concerning your city officials in your city and state now.

_____

_____

_____

_____

_____

_____

_____

_____

_____

_____

_____

_____

_____

_____

_____

DAY 12
Finances & Debt Cancellation

Father in the name of Jesus, as your Word says in Deuteronomy 1:11, And may the Lord, the God of your ancestors, multiply you a thousand times more and bless (**church name**) and my family as he promised.

Father in the name of Jesus, we, the members of (**church name**), take pleasure in our prosperity according to Psalm 35:27.

Father, as we give, it shall be given back to us good measure, pressed down and shaken together and poured in (**church name**)'s lap in the name of Jesus.

I bind the spirit of lack, procrastination, not enough, poverty and hardship in (**church name**) in the name of Jesus. Father God, you said in your Word according to Romans 13:8, owe no man anything except to love one another.

I come against the wicked borrows that do not pay back. We decree and declare the righteous in (**church name**) are generous givers according to Psalm 37:21.

I decree and declare according to Isaiah 48:17 our leader in (**church name**) teaches us to prosper in the name of Jesus.

I decree and declare according to 3 John 2, God's will for (**church name**) and every member to prosper in the name of Jesus.

I decree and declare debt cancelation and restoration for (**church name**) and every member according to Nehemiah 5:1-13 in the name of Jesus.

Father in the name of Jesus, I break all curses of lack, debt and poverty of each member of (**church name**). You are Jehovah-Jireh according to Genesis 22:14, Lord provide for each of us at (**church name**). Rebuke the devourer for (**church name**) and every member of (**church name**)'s sake in the name of Jesus. Command your blessing upon (**church name**) and every member of (**church name**). Lord teach my (**pastor's name**) to profit and lead him/her in the way they should in Jesus' name. Amen.

Prayer Reflection

Now that the Holy Spirit is stirring within you, it is your opportunity for the Holy Spirit to flow prophetically through you. Write what He is saying concerning your finances and personal debt now.

_____

_____

_____

_____

_____

_____

_____

_____

_____

_____

_____

_____

_____

_____

_____

_____

_____

DAY 13
Mental Health

Father in the name of Jesus as your Word says in Luke 10:19, I and every member of (**church name**) has power over the enemy.

Father in the name of Jesus, I believe your Word, that according to John 8:36, whom the son set free is free indeed, that includes (**your pastor's name**), (**church name**) and (**your family name**).

Father God, thank you that you haven't given the members of (**church name**) or (**your name**) the spirit of fear but of power, love and a sound mind according to 2 Timothy 1:7.

Father in the name of Jesus, give (**pastor's name**) and every member of (**church name**) a new heart and mind according to your Word in Ezekiel 36:25-27.

I bind the spirit of anxiety, panic, depression, double-mindedness, insomnia and stress over (**pastor's name**) and every member of (**church name**) in the name of Jesus.

I decree and declare according to the Word in Isaiah 26:3, if we of (**church name**) keep our minds stayed on God, He will keep us in perfect peace in the name of Jesus.

Father in the name of Jesus, I pray (**pastor's name**) will preach deliverance to the captives in (**church name**) and all around the world according to Luke 4:18.

Father in the name of Jesus, we loose ourselves and every member of (**church name**) from all fears including childhood fears, fears from the past, fears from trauma, and fears from our bloodline now, in the name of Jesus.

We are free from the spirit of rape, abuse, abandonment, rejection, incest, accidents, and any genetic deficiencies in the name of Jesus! Amen.

Prayer Reflection

Now that the Holy Spirit is stirring within you, it is your opportunity for the Holy Spirit to flow prophetically through you. Write what He is saying concerning your mental health now.

_____

_____

_____

_____

_____

_____

_____

_____

_____

_____

_____

_____

_____

_____

_____

_____

DAY 14
Unbelieving Spouse & Family Member

Father in the name of Jesus, we believe every unsaved spouse in (**church name**) will be saved. Let your Word come to every unsaved spouse and every member in my family and let them believe.

Father in the name of Jesus, have mercy on my unsaved spouse and let your lovingkindness and tender mercy be over us as a couple.

Father in the name of Jesus, let salvation come to every unsaved spouse in (**church name**) and to (**your name**) household of Obed-Edom according to 2 Samuel 6:11.

I bind and rebuke every demon that has been assigned to every unsaved spouse and family member in (**church name**) to prevent them from receiving salvation.

I decree and declare that every unsaved spouse in (**church name**) and family member rejoices in the Lord's salvation according to Psalm 35:9.

I decree and declare the blinders to be removed from every unsaved spouse and family member of (**church name**) mind in the name of Jesus.

Father in the name of Jesus, you are the God of our salvation and that every unsaved spouse and family member of (**church name**) will be saved according to 1 Chronicles 16:35. Father in the name of Jesus, we confess with our mouths and believe in our hearts that for every unsaved spouse and family member of (**church name**) according to Romans 10:9-10.

Father God, you promised Abraham that through his seed all families of the earth would be blessed, therefore, we at (**church name**) believe and stand on this promise. Thank you, Father, for your protection, salvation, deliverance and healing for every unsaved spouse and family members of (**church name**). Amen.

Prayer Reflection

Now that the Holy Spirit is stirring within you, it is your opportunity for the Holy Spirit to flow prophetically through you. Write what He is saying concerning your unbelieving spouse and/or family member now.

_____

_____

_____

_____

_____

_____

_____

_____

_____

_____

_____

_____

_____

_____

_____

_____

_____

DAY 15
Backsliders

Father in the name of Jesus, we send angels to rescue every lost family member of **(church name)** out of every compromising situation.

Father in the name of Jesus, we pray for every backslider in **(church name)** that they will repent and turn away from their idols and all abominations according to Ezekiel 18:30.

Father in the name of Jesus, help every member of **(church name)** to remember they are a child of God, a saint of God and have a covenant relationship with you.

Father in the name of Jesus, we pray that the light of the gospel will reveal Jesus Christ as Lord and Savior to every member of **(church name)**.

Father in the name of Jesus, we pray every member of **(church name)** will be zealous and repent because you love us and chasten us according to Revelation 3:19.

I decree and declare every member of **(church name)** will repent now of every evil way and evil doing that may dwell in this land that the Lord has given to us and our fathers forever according to Jeremiah 25:5.

Special Note:

Let me remind you we all have challenges in this walk; therefore, backsliders are just necessarily those that have left the church, sometimes it can be us that are in the building every Sunday. Are you guilty of carnality? We can be doubleminded in our walk with God. You can become a backslider by just having unbelief and doubt in your mind. Inconsistency breeds backsliding. You may be backsliding if you have not completely committed your life to Christ. You can't walk with God and stay in the world. Backsliding can simply be a matter of doublemindedness. Yes, prayer warrior and intercessors, I am talking to you.

Prayer Reflection

Now that the Holy Spirit is stirring within you, it is your opportunity for the Holy Spirit to flow prophetically through you. Write what He is saying concerning backsliders now.

_____

_____

_____

_____

_____

_____

_____

_____

_____

_____

_____

_____

_____

_____

_____

_____

_____

DAY 16
Restoration In Families

Father in the name of Jesus, I pray for every church family in (**church name**) to be healed and whole in Jesus' name.

Father God, I pray for healing and forgiveness in my family. Father God wash away the pain of the past in the precious blood of Jesus in (**church name**).

Father in the name of Jesus, I pray according to your Word in Ephesians 4:31-32 we will be kind to one another in (**church name**) and in (**your family**).

Father God let your Word heal every negative word spoken over me and my children(s) lives in the name of Jesus.

Father in the name of Jesus, I pray for healing for every member of (**church name**) who have been physically, sexually, verbally and emotionally abused by family or friends in the name of Jesus. Father, you said in your Word 2 Corinthians 5:7, "Therefore, if anyone is in Christ, he is a new creation. The old has passed away; behold, the new has come."

I bind the spirit of rejection, pain, sorrow, bitterness, and unforgiveness out of our hearts in the name of Jesus.

I bind all mind control bondages and heavy burdens of family destruction, condemnation and abandonment in the name of Jesus.

Father in the name of Jesus, help every member of (**church name**) to forget those things which are behind, and reach for your promises for a bright and healthy future by walking in purpose for (**your name**) life according to Philippians 3:13.

Prayer Reflection

Now that the Holy Spirit is stirring within you, it is your opportunity for the Holy Spirit to flow prophetically through you. Write what He is saying concerning restoration in your family now.

_____

_____

_____

_____

_____

_____

_____

_____

_____

_____

_____

_____

_____

_____

_____

_____

_____

DAY 17

Healing of Sickness & Disease

Father in the name of Jesus, I curse at the root every sickness, disease, pain, virus and infirmity against (**pastor's name**) and every member of (**church name**).

Father in the name of Jesus, I pray that (**pastor's name**) and every member of (**church name**) is healed by Jesus's stripes according to your Word in 1 Peter 2:24.

I pray the prayer of Faith for our (**church name**) that everyone should live and not die according to your Word in Psalms 118:17, we will proclaim the name of the Lord.

I break the neck and cast out any spirits of cancer that would attempt to establish itself in any member of (**church name**) and (**pastor's name**) in the name of Jesus.

I bind any spirits in our lungs, bones, breast, throat, kidneys, stomach, back, spine, skin and liver according to your Word in Psalms 103:3 in the name of Jesus.

I decree and declare that every member of (**church name**) is loosed from the bondage of infirmity in the name of Jesus.

I decree and declare that our bodies at (**church name**) is the Holy temple of God and He is glorified by our total deliverance and healing in the name of Jesus.

Father in the name of Jesus every member of (**church name**) is healed of ever sickness and disease according to your Word in Matthew 9:35.

Father in the name of Jesus, thank you that (**church name**) is whole, of sound mind and body. Thank you, Father God, that we are reenergized, purified, transformed, renewed, strengthened and sanctified for God Almighty. Amen.

Prayer Reflection

Now that the Holy Spirit is stirring within you, it is your opportunity for the Holy Spirit to flow prophetically through you. Write what He is saying concerning your healing in your body now.

_____

_____

_____

_____

_____

_____

_____

_____

_____

_____

_____

_____

_____

_____

_____

_____

_____

DAY 18
Wives

Father in the name of Jesus, I pray for every wife in **(church name).**

Father in the name of Jesus, I pray every wife in **(church name)** is a virtuous woman and a crown to her husband.

Father in the name of Jesus, I pray every wife is submissive to their husband according to 1 Corinthians 11:3 But I want you to understand that the head of every man is Christ, the head of a wife is her husband, and the head of Christ is God in the name of Jesus. (Do you want 'in the name of Jesus' twice in this section?)

Father in the name of Jesus, I pray every wife in **(church name)** will build her house according to Proverbs 14:1; he wisest of women builds her house, but folly with her own hands tears it down.

Father in the name of Jesus, every wife according to Proverbs 31:26 opens her mouth with wisdom, and the teaching of kindness is on her tongue.

I break the neck and cast out any spirits of bitterness, unforgiveness and resentment itself in any wife of **(church name)** in the name of Jesus.

Father in the name of Jesus, heal, set free, deliver, and restore every wife in **(church name)** that have been hurt, abused, offended, or rejected by their husband in the name of Jesus.

We bind the spirit of envy, jealousy, loneliness, competition, isolation, insecurity and low self-esteem for every wife in the name of Jesus.

We loose God's agape love, support, freedom, healing, confidence and God's righteousness in every wife in **(church name)** in the name of Jesus.

Prayer Reflection

Now that the Holy Spirit is stirring within you, it is your opportunity for the Holy Spirit to flow prophetically through you. Write what He is saying concerning your marriage or you individually as a wife now.

_____

_____

_____

_____

_____

_____

_____

_____

_____

_____

_____

_____

_____

_____

_____

_____

DAY 19
Church Growth

Father in the name of Jesus, we pray for church growth in **(church name)** according to Acts 2:47. **(Church name)** is praising God and having favor with all the people because the Lord added to the number day by day of those being saved in **(church name)** in Jesus' name.

Father in the name of Jesus, we pray that the fivefold ministry gifts will arise in (church name) in the name of Jesus. Your Word says in Ephesians 4:11-12, you gave the apostles, the prophets, the evangelist, the shepherds and teachers to equip the saints for the work of ministry for building up the body of Christ, therefore it is so in (church name) in the name of Jesus.

Father in the name of Jesus, we decree that **(church name)** is coming together in prayer according to Acts 1:14 for church growth in the name of Jesus.

Father in the name of Jesus, we decree according to 1 Peter 2:2, Like newborn infants, long for the pure spiritual milk, that members of **(church name)** may grow up into salvation in the name of Jesus.

Father in the name of Jesus, we decree according to Acts 5:14, and more than ever believers were added to the Lord, multitudes of both men and women in **(church name)** in the name of Jesus.

We decree and declare in growth in every ministry in **(church name)** according to 2 Peter 3:18. Every member of **(church name)** is growing in grace and knowledge of the Lord and Savior Jesus Christ to serve in and on ministries together in the name of Jesus.

We decree and declare growth in tithes & offerings in **(church name).**

We decree and declare growth in membership in **(church name).**

We decree and declare growth in finances in **(church name).**

We decree and declare growth in discipleship in **(church name).**

Prayer Reflection

Now that the Holy Spirit is stirring within you, it is your opportunity for the Holy Spirit to flow prophetically through you. Write what He is saying concerning church growth in your local assembly now.

_____

_____

_____

_____

_____

_____

_____

_____

_____

_____

_____

_____

_____

_____

_____

_____

_____

DAY 20
Youth

Father in the name of Jesus, our children at (**church name**) do not put their trust in human wisdom but in the power of God.

Father in the name of Jesus, teach our children at (**church name**) wisdom ways and lead them in straight paths according to your Word in Proverbs 4:11.

Father in the name of Jesus, we cancel every strategy and operation designated to destroy our children at (**church name**).

Father in name of Jesus, we pray that every youth in (**church name**) are surrounded with grace, mercy and favor.

I decree and declare that our youth at (**church name**) are being transformed right now by the renewing of their minds according to your Word in Romans 12:2.

I decree and declare our youth of (**church name**) are successful, intelligent, respectful and spirit filled in the name of Jesus.

I bind the spirit of drugs, violence, teen pregnancy, peer pressure, gang affiliation, rape, and rejection from our youth at (**church name**). Thank you, Father God, they will never settle for anything less than their inheritance provides, in Jesus' name. Amen.

Prayer Reflection

Now that the Holy Spirit is stirring within you, it is your opportunity for the Holy Spirit to flow prophetically through you. Write what He is saying concerning our youth now.

_____

_____

_____

_____

_____

_____

_____

_____

_____

_____

_____

_____

_____

_____

_____

_____

DAY 21
First Family

Father in the name of Jesus, we decree the blood of Jesus over (**first family name**) in the name of Jesus.

Father in the name of Jesus, we decree the (**first family name**) is protected from hurt, harm, danger, and accidents according to 2 Thessalonians 3:13 in the name of Jesus.

Father, thank you for establishing and guarding the (**first family name**) against the evil one according to your Word.

Father in the name of Jesus, we decree the (**first family name**) is of one heart and on one accord in the name of Jesus.

Father in the name of Jesus, we thank you that the (**first family name**) is healed from any sickness or disease, poverty and lack, fear, and oppression in the name of Jesus.

Father in the name of Jesus, we decree and declare the (**first family name**) is covered in the blood of Jesus with your blessings, favor and strength in the name of Jesus.

Father in the name of Jesus, we decree, unity with the (**first family name**) marriage and amongst their child(ren) in the name of Jesus.

We bind the spirit of divorce, separation and discord in (**first family name**) in the name of Jesus.

Father in the name of Jesus, we decree according to Psalm 103:3, healing and restoration to the (**first family name**) bodies in the name of Jesus.

We decree and declare perfect health for all members of (**first family name**).

We decree and declare wholeness in every area of their marriage, children, finances, and health in the name of Jesus.

Prayer Reflection

Now that the Holy Spirit is stirring within you, it is your opportunity for the Holy Spirit to flow prophetically through you. Write what He is saying concerning the first family now.

_____

_____

_____

_____

_____

_____

_____

_____

_____

_____

_____

_____

_____

_____

_____

_____

DAY 22
Employment

Father in the name of Jesus, we pray for employment and stability for every member of **(church name)** in the name of Jesus.

Father in the name of Jesus, we decree according to Jeremiah 29:11, For You Lord know the plans you have, plans for good and not for evil, to give each member of **(church name)** a future and a hope in the name of Jesus.

Father in the name of Jesus, help every member of **(church name)** to seek first the Kingdom of God and your righteousness, and all these things will be added unto us according to Matthew 6:33 in the name of Jesus.

Father in the name of Jesus, we decree employment and promotion for every member of **(church name)** according to Psalms 75:6 in the name of Jesus.

Father in the name of Jesus, we decree careers, entrepreneurship, internships, and promotions with every member of **(church name)** in the name of Jesus.

We bind the spirit of slothfulness.

We bind the spirit of laziness.

We bind the spirit of lack.

We bind the spirit of not enough.

We bind the spirit of poverty and poverty mindsets.

We loose the spirit of abundance.

We loose a renewed mindset.

We loose overflow.

We loose prosperity.

We loose motivation.

We loose confidence.

We loose skillset.

Prayer Reflection

Now that the Holy Spirit is stirring within you, it is your opportunity for the Holy Spirit to flow prophetically through you. Write what He is saying concerning your personal employment now.

_____

_____

_____

_____

_____

_____

_____

_____

_____

_____

_____

_____

_____

_____

_____

DAY 23
Women

Father in the name of Jesus, I pray for every woman in **(church name).**

Father in the name of Jesus, I pray every woman in **(church name)** is a virtuous woman in the name of Jesus.

Father in the name of Jesus, I pray every woman in **(church name)** doesn't throw away their confidence according to Hebrews 10:35 because there is a great recompence of a reward in the name of Jesus.

Father in the name of Jesus, I pray every woman in **(church name)** will build her house according to Proverbs 14:1; he wisest of women builds her house, but folly with her own hands tears it down.

Father in the name of Jesus, every woman according to Proverbs 31:26 opens her mouth with wisdom, and the teaching of kindness is on her tongue to her children, business and family in (church name) in the name of Jesus.

I break the neck and cast out any spirits of bitterness, unforgiveness and resentment itself in any woman of **(church name)** in the name of Jesus.

Father in the name of Jesus heal, set free, deliver, and restore every woman in **(church name)** that have been hurt, abused, offended, or rejected by their family, friends, church members, ex-husbands, husband, or boyfriends in the name of Jesus.

We bind the spirit of envy, jealousy, loneliness, competition, isolation, insecurity, anger, bitterness, and low self-esteem for every woman in the name of Jesus.

We loose God's agape love, support, peace, humility, freedom, healing, confidence and God's righteousness in every woman in **(church name)** in the name of Jesus.

Prayer Reflection

Now that the Holy Spirit is stirring within you, it is your opportunity for the Holy Spirit to flow prophetically through you. Write what He is saying concerning you as a woman now.

_____

_____

_____

_____

_____

_____

_____

_____

_____

_____

_____

_____

_____

_____

_____

DAY 24
Education

Father in the name of Jesus, we decree education and higher education for every member of **(church name)** old and young in the name of Jesus.

Father in the name of Jesus, we decree according to Proverbs 16:16. How much better to get wisdom than gold in the name of Jesus.

Father in the name of Jesus, we decree according to 2 Timothy 3:7 that every member of **(church name)** are always learning and able to arrive at a knowledge of the truth in the name of Jesus.

Father in the name of Jesus, we bind the spirit of fear according to 2 Timothy 1:7 for every member of **(church name)** and we loose confidence to obtain higher education in the name of Jesus.

We thank you Father God, that nothing is impossible with you according to Luke 1:37 in the name of Jesus.

We decree and declare scholarships.

We decree and declare grants.

We decree and declare work study programs.

We decree and declare affordable schools.

We decree and declare free community and local education.

Prayer Reflection

Now that the Holy Spirit is stirring within you, it is your opportunity for the Holy Spirit to flow prophetically through you. Write what He is saying concerning your education now.

_____

_____

_____

_____

_____

_____

_____

_____

_____

_____

_____

_____

_____

_____

_____

_____

DAY 25
Breaking Curses

Father in the name of Jesus, we pray every negative generational curse be broken from every member of **(church name)** in the name of Jesus.

Father in the name of Jesus, we pray according to Isaiah 58:12 for every member of **(church name)** in the name of Jesus.

Father in the name of Jesus, we thank you that we at **(church name)** are redeemed from the curse of the law according to Galatians 3:13 in the name of Jesus.

Father in the name of Jesus, we decree every family in **(church name)** is blessed according to Genesis 12:3 in the name of Jesus.

We bind all written and spoken curses that would affect our lives in **(church name)** in the name of Jesus.

We bind all generational curses of lust, perversion, witchcraft, rejection, rebellion, and fear in every member of **(church name)** in the name of Jesus.

We bind all curses on our finances at **(church name)** in the name of Jesus.

We loose ourselves in **(church name)** from any evil inheritance NOW in the name of Jesus.

We loose ourselves in **(church name)** from sickness, ungodly lifestyles, lesbianism and homosexuality according to you Psalm 34:17. When the righteous cry for help, the Lord hears and delivers them out of all their troubles in the name of Jesus.

Latasha R. Brown

Prayer Reflection

Now that the Holy Spirit is stirring within you, it is your opportunity for the Holy Spirit to flow prophetically through you. Write what He is saying concerning breaking curses now.

_____

_____

_____

_____

_____

_____

_____

_____

_____

_____

_____

_____

_____

_____

_____

DAY 26
Deliverance of Ungodly Soul Ties

Father in the name of Jesus, we decree and declare you are delivering every member of **(church name)** from ungodly soul ties in the name of Jesus.

Father in the name of Jesus, we bind ungodly associations that has caused evil spirits to be transferred in the name of Jesus.

Father in the name of Jesus, we loose our minds in **(church name)** from all spirits of control, mental bondage, insanity, fantasy, and lusted in the name of Jesus.

Father in the name of Jesus, we decree and declare our minds in **(church name)** are free as your word says in Proverbs 23:7, for as he thinks in his heart, in the name of Jesus.

We loose ourselves in **(church name)** from the powers of Jezebel according to 1 Kings 21:23 in Jesus' name.

We bind every assignment and curse of Jezebel and spirits operating in the bloodline of every member in **(church name)** in the name of Jesus.

We bind all spirit marriages that would cause incubus and succubus demons to attack our lives in **(church name)** in the name of Jesus.

We decree and declare that we in **(church name)** have a covenant with God through the blood of Jesus Christ. We in **(church name)** are joined to the Lord and we are one spirit with Him in the name of Jesus.

We bind all ungodly covenants and renew our covenant in **(church name)** to God through the body and blood of Jesus in His name.

We bind the spirit of whoredoms in **(church name)** according to your Word in Hosea 4:12 in the name of Jesus.

Prayer Reflection

Now that the Holy Spirit is stirring within you, it is your opportunity for the Holy Spirit to flow prophetically through you. Write what He is saying concerning deliverance with ungodly soul ties in your life now.

_____

_____

_____

_____

_____

_____

_____

_____

_____

_____

_____

_____

_____

_____

_____

_____

_____

_____

DAY 27
The Glory

Father in the name of Jesus, we decree and declare that your Glory is resting in **(church name)** in the name of Jesus.

Father in the name of Jesus, we pray according to 2 Chronicles 5:14, "for the Glory of the Lord has filled the house of God" in **(church name)** in the name of Jesus.

Father in the name of Jesus, we loose the radiance, splendor and beauty of Glory in **(church name)** in the name of Jesus.

Father in the name of Jesus, we decree and declare that every member of **(church name)** and **(pastor's name)** is called to your Glory as your Word says in 1 Thessalonians 2:12 in the name of Jesus.

We loose your angels to live in **(church name)** with thunder and lightning will manifest in **(church name)** according to Revelation 18:1 in Jesus' name.

Father in the name of Jesus, let the Glory rest in each worship service in **(church name)** Sunday after Sunday in the name of Jesus.

Father in the name of Jesus, let your Glory rest upon **(pastor's name),** first family, ministers, deacons, leadership in **(church name)** in the name of Jesus.

Father in the name of Jesus, we decree and declare the Glory shall rest on the praise and worship, the teaching and preaching, the salvation of the lost and our tithes and offering at **(church name)** according to Romans 8:17 in the name of Jesus.

Prayer Reflection

Now that the Holy Spirit is stirring within you, it is your opportunity for the Holy Spirit to flow prophetically through you. Write what He is saying concerning the Glory of God in your life now.

_____

_____

_____

_____

_____

_____

_____

_____

_____

_____

_____

_____

_____

_____

_____

_____

DAY 28
Prosperity

Father in the name of Jesus, we decree and declare you are taking pleasure in every member of **(church name)** according to Psalm 35:27 in the name of Jesus.

Father in the name of Jesus, we pray a great blessing of prosperity resides in **(church name)** and the community of our church in the name of Jesus.

Father in the name of Jesus, we bind lack, poverty, emptiness, barrenness, and oppression in **(church name)** in the name of Jesus.

Father in the name of Jesus, we loose wealth, power, abundance, wisdom, and sufficiency in every member of **(church name)** in the name of Jesus.

Father in the name of Jesus, we decree and declare **(pastor's name)** and every member of **(church name)** possess the land which the Lord swore unto our fathers, Abraham, Isaac and Jacob according to Deuteronomy 1:8 in Jesus' name.

Father in the name of Jesus, multiply **(church name)** in church growth, outreach servants, tithes and offerings, budgets, ministry help, and administration according to your Word in Deuteronomy 11:21 in the name of Jesus.

Father in the name of Jesus, increase **(pastor's name)** and comfort on every side according to your Word in Psalm 71:21 in the name of Jesus.

Father in the name of Jesus, we decree and declare that every member of **(church name)** will seek ye first the kingdom of God, and His righteousness, therefore, all these things shall be added unto you according to your Word in Matthew 6:33 in the name of Jesus.

Prayer Reflection

Now that the Holy Spirit is stirring within you, it is your opportunity for the Holy Spirit to flow prophetically through you. Write what He is saying concerning obtaining and sustaining prosperity in your life now.

_____

_____

_____

_____

_____

_____

_____

_____

_____

_____

_____

_____

_____

_____

DAY 29
Tithing

Father in the name of Jesus, we decree and declare that every member of **(church name)** are 100% tithers in the name of Jesus.

Father in the name of Jesus, we decree and declare according to Deuteronomy 14:22, that we in **(church name)** tithe all the increase of they (Should 'they' be 'the'?) seed in the name of Jesus.

Father in the name of Jesus, we decree and declare that we are cheerful givers in **(church name)** according to 2 Corinthians 9:7 in the name of Jesus.

Father in the name of Jesus, help us in **(church name)** to honor you Lord with our wealth and with the first fruits of all our produce according to Proverbs 3:9-10, so that our barns shall be filled in the name of Jesus.

Father in the name of Jesus, let every member of **(church name)** offer right sacrifices and put our trust in you Lord according to your Word in Psalm 4:5 in the name of Jesus.

We bind every religious, stingy and robbing spirit that tries to attack members in **(church name)** in the name of Jesus. We loose a giving and loving spirit to bring our full tithe in the storehouse of **(church name)** so that there may be food in our homes in the name of Jesus according to Malachi 3:8-10.

Father in the name of Jesus, we decree and declare that every member of **(church name)** is giving tithes of all that they receive, that includes child support, alimony, gifts, etc. according to Luke 18:12 in the name of Jesus.

Prayer Reflection

Now that the Holy Spirit is stirring within you, it is your opportunity for the Holy Spirit to flow prophetically through you. Write what He is saying concerning Tithing in your life now.

_____

_____

_____

_____

_____

_____

_____

_____

_____

_____

_____

_____

_____

_____

_____

_____

DAY 30
Wisdom

Father in the name of Jesus, we decree and declare the seven-fold anointing to rest upon our leader. We release the spirit of wisdom, understanding, knowledge, counsel, might, fear of the Lord and the Spirit of the Lord to rest upon on **(pastor's name)** now according to Isaiah 11:2 in the name of Jesus.

Father in the name of Jesus, we decree and declare that every member of **(church name)** that you will lead us in the way we should go in our everyday lives according to Isaiah 48:17 in the name of Jesus.

Father in the name of Jesus, we decree and declare according to John 16:13 that every member in **(church name)** we be led by the Spirit of truth in the name of Jesus.

Father in the name of Jesus, we decree and declare that every member in **(church name)** according to Proverbs 3:6 will acknowledge you and you will direct our paths with our families, finances and faith in the name of Jesus.

Father in the name of Jesus, we decree and declare you Lord will instruct us, lead us and teach us in **(church name)** according to Psalm 32:8 in the name of Jesus.

Father in the name of Jesus, let every member of **(church name)** hear your voice and a stranger's voice we will not follow according to John 10:27 in the name of Jesus.

Father in the name of Jesus, don't let anyone in **(church name)** lack wisdom. We decree and declare according to James 1:5-7 to ask in faith for wisdom concerning every area of our lives in the name of Jesus.

Prayer Reflection

Now that the Holy Spirit is stirring within you, it is your opportunity for the Holy Spirit to flow prophetically through you. Write what He is saying concerning wisdom in your life now.

_____

_____

_____

_____

_____

_____

_____

_____

_____

_____

_____

_____

_____

_____

_____

DAY 31

Holy Spirit

Father in the name of Jesus, we decree and declare that every member of **(church name)** is led by Holy Spirit in the name of Jesus.

Father in the name of Jesus, pour out your Holy Spirit upon **(church name)** every time we gather together according to Acts 2:38 in the name of Jesus.

Father in the name of Jesus, let every member of **(church name)** possess the fruit of the spirit in their lives according to Galatians 5:22-23. We loose the fruit of love, joy, patience, kindness, goodness, faithfulness, gentleness and self-control over every member, minister, elder, deacon, youth and leadership in **(church name)** in the name of Jesus.

Father in the name of Jesus, we decree and declare according to John 14:26, that we in **(church name)** will receive the Helper-Holy Spirit to teach us all things and bring to our remembrance all that you Lord have said on our behalf in the name of Jesus.

Father in the name of Jesus, we decree and declare that we are cheerful givers in **(church name)** according to 2 Corinthians 9:7 in the name of Jesus.

Father in the name of Jesus, help us in **(church name)** to build ourselves up praying in Holy Spirit for our pastor, families, church leadership and community according to Jude 1:20 in the name of Jesus.

Father in the name of Jesus, we decree and declare according to Acts 2:17 that you are pouring out your Spirit on all flesh in **(church name)** so your sons and your daughters in **(church name)** shall prophesy and your young men shall see visions and your old men shall dream dreams in the name of Jesus.

Prayer Reflection

Now that the Holy Spirit is stirring within you, it is your opportunity for the Holy Spirit to flow prophetically through you. Write what He is saying concerning your life now.

_____

_____

_____

_____

_____

_____

_____

_____

_____

_____

_____

_____

_____

_____

_____

_____

About the Author

Latasha R. Brown is the 1st Lady of Abundant Blessings Church, licensed minister, mental health practitioner, prophetic counselor, intercessor and founder of "Girlfriend In God Ministries" based in Chicago, IL. She currently holds a master's degree (with Distinction) in Counseling Psychology from North Park University. She serves alongside her husband, Pastor Clarence E. Brown III in teaching the Word of God.

Aside from ministering God's Word in her local church, Latasha R. Brown speaks at seminars, workshops and conferences dedicated to women all over. She also leads a weekly women's prayer line. She is a coach, mentor, entrepreneur, and transformational leader passionate about helping equip and enrich the lives of women.

TO CONTACT THE AUTHOR:

Latasha R. Brown

Website - www.LatashaRbrown.com

Facebook - Latasha R. Brown Ministries

Instagram - @ladylatashab

Twitter - @ladylatashab

Email - Advancingthefamily@gmail.com

Prayer Reflection

Now that the Holy Spirit is stirring within you, it is your opportunity for the Holy Spirit to flow prophetically through you. Write what He is saying concerning your life and the life of those around you.

_____

_____

_____

_____

_____

_____

_____

_____

_____

_____

_____

_____

_____

_____

Prayer Reflection

Now that the Holy Spirit is stirring within you, it is your opportunity for the Holy Spirit to flow prophetically through you. Write what He is saying concerning your life and the life of those around you.

_____

_____

_____

_____

_____

_____

_____

_____

_____

_____

_____

_____

_____

_____

_____

_____

Prayer Reflection

Now that the Holy Spirit is stirring within you, it is your opportunity for the Holy Spirit to flow prophetically through you. Write what He is saying concerning your life and the life of those around you.

_____

_____

_____

_____

_____

_____

_____

_____

_____

_____

_____

_____

_____

_____

_____

Prayer Reflection

Now that the Holy Spirit is stirring within you, it is your opportunity for the Holy Spirit to flow prophetically through you. Write what He is saying concerning your life and the life of those around you.

_____

_____

_____

_____

_____

_____

_____

_____

_____

_____

_____

_____

_____

_____

_____

_____

Prayer Reflection

Now that the Holy Spirit is stirring within you, it is your opportunity for the Holy Spirit to flow prophetically through you. Write what He is saying concerning your life and the life of those around you.

_____

_____

_____

_____

_____

_____

_____

_____

_____

_____

_____

_____

_____

_____

Prayer Reflection

Now that the Holy Spirit is stirring within you, it is your opportunity for the Holy Spirit to flow prophetically through you. Write what He is saying concerning your life and the life of those around you.

_____

_____

_____

_____

_____

_____

_____

_____

_____

_____

_____

_____

_____

_____

_____

_____

Prayer Reflection

Now that the Holy Spirit is stirring within you, it is your opportunity for the Holy Spirit to flow prophetically through you. Write what He is saying concerning your life and the life of those around you.

_____

_____

_____

_____

_____

_____

_____

_____

_____

_____

_____

_____

_____

_____

Prayer Reflection

Now that the Holy Spirit is stirring within you, it is your opportunity for the Holy Spirit to flow prophetically through you. Write what He is saying concerning your life and the life of those around you.

_____

_____

_____

_____

_____

_____

_____

_____

_____

_____

_____

_____

_____

_____

_____

Prayer Reflection

Now that the Holy Spirit is stirring within you, it is your opportunity for the Holy Spirit to flow prophetically through you. Write what He is saying concerning your life and the life of those around you.

_____

_____

_____

_____

_____

_____

_____

_____

_____

_____

_____

_____

_____

Prayer Reflection

Now that the Holy Spirit is stirring within you, it is your opportunity for the Holy Spirit to flow prophetically through you. Write what He is saying concerning your life and the life of those around you.

_____

_____

_____

_____

_____

_____

_____

_____

_____

_____

_____

_____

_____

_____

Prayer Reflection

Now that the Holy Spirit is stirring within you, it is your opportunity for the Holy Spirit to flow prophetically through you. Write what He is saying concerning your life and the life of those around you.

_____

_____

_____

_____

_____

_____

_____

_____

_____

_____

_____

_____

_____

_____

Made in the USA
Columbia, SC
28 September 2023

23529231R00057